A MEIRIONNYDD COAST WALK

A MEIRIONNYDD COAST WALK

by

Laurence Main

© *Text: Laurence Main*

Copyright © by Gwasg Carreg Gwalch 2001.

ISBN: 0-86381-666-5

Cover design: Alan Jones

First published in 2001 by
Gwasg Carreg Gwalch, 12 Iard yr Orsaf, Llanrwst, Wales LL26 0EH
℡ 01492 642031   ▤ 01492 641502
✆ books@carreg-gwalch.co.uk   Internet: www.carreg-gwalch.co.uk

About the Author:
A Meirionnydd Coast Walk is Laurence Main's 49th walking guidebook. His 50th, *Walks Between Bus Stops in Gwynedd*, will also be published by Gwasg Carreg Gwalch. Earlier titles include *A Guide to the Dyfi Valley Way, In the Footsteps of King Arthur* and *The Spirit Paths of Wales*. Laurence Main has lived in Meirionnydd since 1981 and is the Chairman of the Ramblers' Association's Footpaths Committee in Meirionnydd.

A day's walking; a week's good health.'
(French proverb)

Contents

Acknowledgements

Great care has been taken to be accurate. The publishers cannot, however, accept responsibility for any errors which may appear, or their consequences.

This walk is along rights of way, including unclassified county roads. An agreed diversion, using the ladder-stile, is followed around Pen-isa'r-cwm (mile 45), while the path across Barmouth Bridge (mile 29) has a toll. Dogs are never welcome on sheep pastures. It is essential that you follow the Country Code. Please remember that you cross private land as a privilege, so do not spoil it for those who may follow you.

James Webb, a member of the Meirionnydd Local Group of the Ramblers' Association, accompanied me along part of this route. Dr H Van der Helm-Hylkema, a Dutch psychologist, contacted me about the strange light she saw at the stone circle at grid ref. SH 611218 (between miles 36 and 37). An anonymous collector of tolls (free for walkers!) on the bridge over the Afon Dwyryd (mile 66) quenched my thirst with a (free) drink on the hottest day of the year after I had walked from Harlech. David Coleman of Gwynedd Council cheerfully answered my queries about rights of way, which are generally in good order and signed on this route. The public libraries at Dolgellau and Machynlleth proved invaluable for research. Paul Devereux led me to research the lights associated with the Mary Jones mission between December 1904 and July 1905. Most of all, I must thank the railway being there to provide access to the route. The scenic Cambrian Coast Line is a great asset which deserves the support of all 'green' tourists.

Introduction

Wales has a coast that has much to offer the walker. In places, especially in Pembrokeshire, it can be admired at close quarters from spectacular clifftop paths. The section between the estuaries of the Dyfi and the Glaslyn that is occupied by Meirionnydd is overlooked by impressive mountains. Their foothills, at least, demand a visit from the pedestrian tourist eager to gain sweeping views.

There is much of interest to seek out. Ancient stone circles and standing stones abound, bearing witness to the interest our prehistoric ancestors had in this area. Set foot along these paths and you may follow in the footsteps of Branwen, one of the Three Matriarchs of Britain and the fairest maiden in the world, as she wandered from her brother Bendigeidfran's court at Harlech before Matholwch's ships appeared from Ireland.

Delightful rivers tumble down to the sea through valleys where the native oak woodland has escaped the plough. Stone walls add character to the higher pasture, where it seems you have only the birds of Rhiannon to commune with. At intervals, just when they are welcome, come the little resorts with their welcome facilities. Barmouth may appear to be twinned with Blackpool, but it doesn't take long to climb above its sands into the most rugged of landscapes. And Blackpool doesn't have a railway bridge spanning the Mawddach estuary.

A splendid castle, preserved slate caverns, ruins of old lead mines, ancient churches, a chapel that featured in a most notorious painting, an Italianate village which became the location for a television series, the scene of a murder and the narrow-gauge railways for which Wales is so famous are all here.

The paths are good and access to them by public transport is superior to similar areas of unspoilt countryside. The Cambrian Coast Line isn't just one of the best train rides in Britain. It has retained its many little halts. In an answer to a rambler's prayer, it enables linear walks to be enjoyed in an unparalleled way. Linear walks can be made short or long, to suit your walking appetite. There are plenty of stations to choose to stop at. Cheap ranger tickets are available. There are even bus services to complement the trains. Why drive a car here?

There is no need to backpack. Heavy burdens can be left in a hotel, youth hostel or tent, while the whole route is walked in a series of day-trips from a single base. There are plenty of campsites close to railway stations or bus stops. Tourist Information Centres provide comprehensive coverage. Merry Meirionnydd really does welcome pedestrian tourists.

When devising this route, I bore in mind that it can be a link in the chain of walking routes around Wales. The Dyfi Valley Way meets this route at Aberdyfi. It can take you to Borth, where Liz Allan's Cardigan Bay Coast Walk leads south to join the Pembrokeshire Coast Path. John Cantrell has described a Lleyn Peninsula Coast Path if you wish to proceed north of Porthmadog towards Caernarfon, and so on . . . If you're hooked on long distance walking, keep up to date with the directory on long distance paths published by the Long Distance Walkers' Association.

This Meirionnydd Coast Walk is a fine walking holiday in itself. It can be divided into eight sections, to suit a week's holiday. This guidebook consists of a detailed strip map at a generous scale, marking stiles, gates and signposts. The mileage is shown from the start, while a continuous gradient profile gives an impression of how demanding the walk is. The map is intended to face the direction of the walk from south to north (and can easily be reversed). This means that north cannot always be at the top of the page, so do check the direction of north as indicated on each page. The numbers of the relevant Ordnance Survey maps are also given (plus grid references for the start and finish of each section). The whole route of 72 miles is on just two Ordnance Survey Outdoor Leisure maps (nos. 18 and 23). These are recommended so that the strip map can be related to the surrounding countryside.

It is hoped to waymark this route with a distinctive turtle symbol (the world's largest turtle was washed ashore at Harlech in 1989).

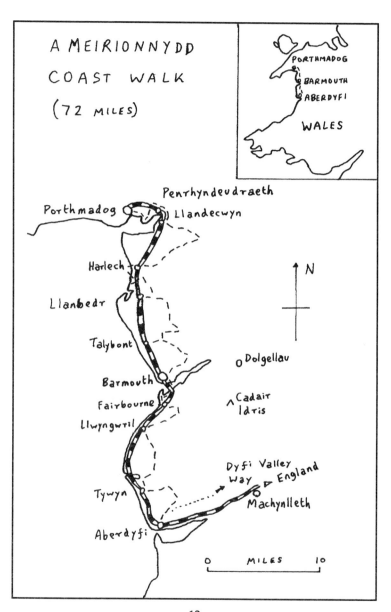

A MEIRIONNYDD
COAST WALK
(72 MILES)

PORTHMADOG
BARMOUTH
ABERDYFI
WALES

Penrhyndeudraeth
Porthmadog
Llandecwyn
Harlech
Llanbedr
Talybont
Dolgellau
Barmouth
Cadair Idris
Fairbourne
Llwyngwril
Dyfi Valley Way
England
Tywyn
Machynlleth
Aberdyfi

N

0   MILES   10

12

Aberdyfi – Tywyn

Aberdyfi must often have been the target for long distance walkers in the days when Shank's Pony was the normal mode of transport. The locals point to a Roman road occupying a rocky ledge above the Dyfi. One variation of Sarn Helen may have come this way. Its position on the northern, Gwynedd, shore of the Dyfi gives the village a strategic importance. The Dyfi provides Powys (just a few miles inland) with that princedom's only outlet to a sea. Ceredigion (part of old Dyfed) is on the southern shore. Aberdyfi was a useful place to meet.

Meirionnydd is named after Meirion, the grandson of Cunedda, who came south from Manaw Gododdin at the end of the Roman era, in the early fifth century. Cunedda drove the Irish out of Gwynedd and divided his new kingdom between his seven sons and Meirion at his death. Meirion's father, Tybion, was Cunedda's firstborn, who died before the move south from Manaw Gododdin. Ceredigion was named after Meirion's uncle Ceredig (one of Cunedda's sons).

By the early sixth century, Gwynedd was ruled by the mighty Maelgwn (Cunedda's great-grandson). He gave his name to the sands opposite Aberdyfi – Traeth Maelgwn. Legend tells of how he won a contest to decide which prince could occupy his throne longest while the tide came in. Maelgwn's chair was prepared with waxed feathers so that it would float more easily. Was this when Maelgwn was declared Pendragon? Was this before or after the death of King Arthur, the previous Pendragon, at the Battle of Camlan (near Dinas Mawddwy) in 537?

Aberdyfi was the scene of several recorded Councils in the Middle Ages, as when the Welsh clergy protested against the influence of Canterbury in 1140 and Llywelyn ap Iorwerth attempted to unite Wales in 1216. Civil war had been more prevalent, resulting in Rhys, Prince of South Wales maintaining a small castle in Aberdyfi from 1151 to 1157. It stood on Pen-y-Bryn (where there is now a shelter known as 'the bandstand'). In the same century, the seductive Nest escaped with her lover Owain ap Cadwgan by boat from here to Ireland.

The sea has played its part in Aberdyfi's history, with the herrings landed at Aberdyfi in the famine year of 1649 feeding the whole of southern Meirionnydd. Pirates based themselves here, with one local tale being of a beautiful lady who gave up her life rather than leave her pirate lover.

Aberdyfi's contact with the sea may only date from around AD 490. Before then, there may well have been a fertile plain in Cardigan Bay. This was the legendary Cantre'r Gwaelod (Lowland Hundred) which may have been drowned in the same catastrophe that turned the single Isle of Scilly on Roman maps into the Scilly Isles. Perhaps there were earthquakes along the west coast of Britain around 490.

Fossil forests on the Ceredigion shore have been dated to about 3500 BC, so the legends may reveal a folk memory of astonishing longevity. Something must have happened before AD 500 too. Go to Penmachno, for example, to discover a church founded by St Tudclyd in the early sixth century (when Maelgwn reigned). This Tudclyd took holy orders to atone for the misdeeds of his father, the very Seithennin the drunkard of the legend. The seaward side of Cantre'r Gwaelod had to be protected from the sea by a wall or dike. This Seithennin failed to maintain these defences and was drunk when a storm broke the wall and the sea flooded the land. A church, complete with bells, was said to have been drowned. This story inspired Charles Dibdin to compose the song *The Bells of Aberdovey* in 1785, as part of his Drury Lane hit *Liberty Hall*.

The Bells of Aberdovey

If thou truly dost love me . . .
As I truly do love thee,
To all who live on land or main,
Say the bells of Aberdovey;
One, two, three, four, five, six,
Join us in a merry strain,
Say the bells of Aberdovey.
Listen to the joyous bells,
While through the meadows straying,
O'er the hills their music swells,
And this is what they're saying:
Pretty maidens come again . . .

Lead, silver, copper and zinc were mined in the Aberdyfi area and exported from its harbour, along with timber from the local oak woodland. Records for the export of minerals exist from 1708, while the final item was the sale of the Corbet Dovey copper mine in 1863. So close was this to the shore that the ore was loaded directly onto the boats.

The railway arrived from Machynlleth in 1867. There was a brief prospect of Aberdyfi becoming a port for Ireland, but its future was to become an Outward Bound Centre and a resort for tourists. Since 1988, Aberdyfi has been a terminal point of the Dyfi Valley Way. This long distance walk of 108 miles goes up the Dyfi Valley to the summit of Aran Fawddwy (2971 ft) and back down the other side of the river to Borth.

As you approach Tywyn, just after mile 9, look out for an ancient standing stone known as Croes Faen. This is said to protect Tywyn from a fiery dragon. Are we on the subject of leys or spirit paths? It also marked the Christian pilgrimage route to St Cadfan's Tywyn. Presumably, it was marked with a cross, although this seems to have vanished. Christians often took over prehistoric monuments.

MAP 1

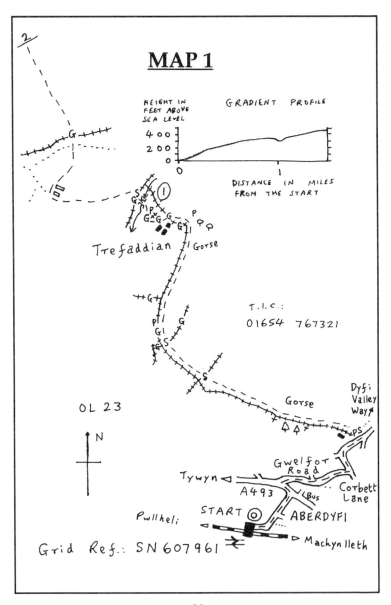

HEIGHT IN
FEET ABOVE
SEA LEVEL

GRADIENT PROFILE

400
200
0

0   1

DISTANCE IN MILES
FROM THE START

Trefaddian Gorse

T.I.C.:
01654 767321

OL 23

N

Gorse

Dyfi
Valley
Way

PS

Gwelfor
Road

Tywyn

A493   Bus

Corbett
Lane

Pwllheli

START   ABERDYFI

Grid Ref.: SN 607961   Machynlleth

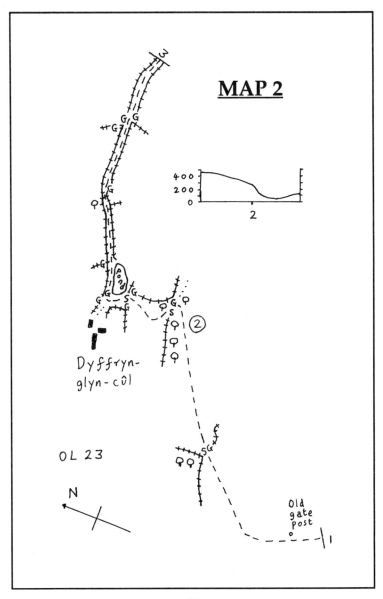

MAP 2

Dyffryn-
glyn-cûl

OL 23

N

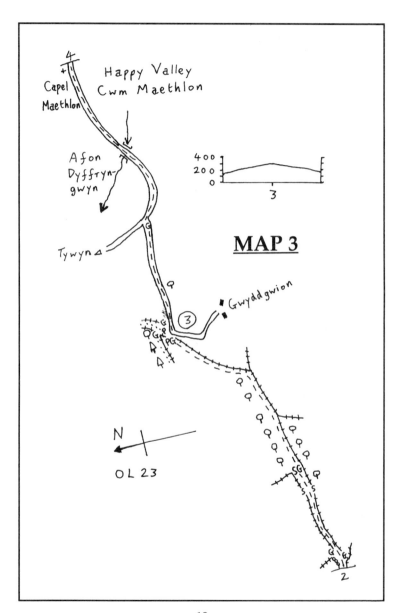

Capel
Maethlon

Happy Valley
Cwm Maethlon

Afon
Dyffryn-
gwyn

Tywyn

400
200
0

3

MAP 3

Gwyddgwion

③

N

OL 23

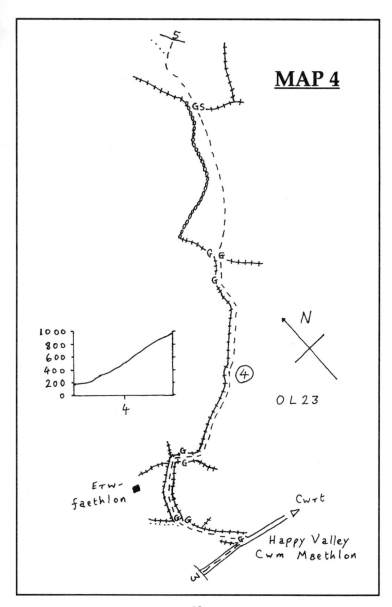

MAP 4

5

GS

G G

G

1000
800
600
400
200
0

4

④

OL 23

N

Erw-
faethlon

G
G

G G

G

Cwrt

Happy Valley
Cwm Maethlon

3

MAP 5

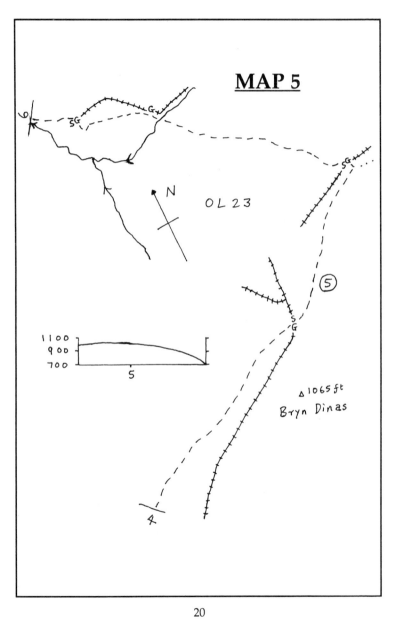

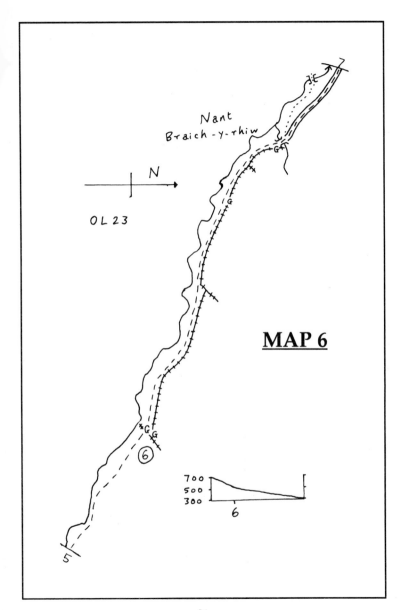

Nant
Braich-y-rhiw

N

OL 23

MAP 6

G

G

G

6

5

700
500
300
6

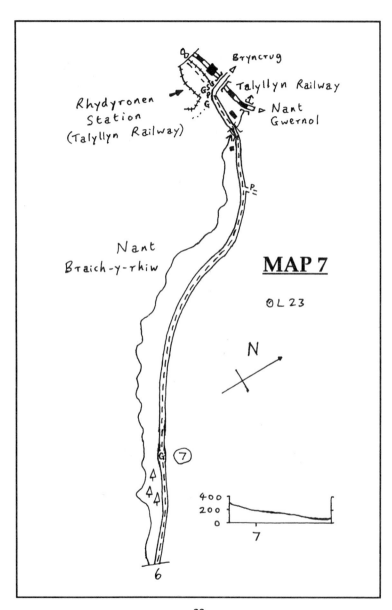

Bryncrug

Talyllyn Railway

Rhydyronen
Station
(Talyllyn Railway)

Nant
Gwernol

Nant
Braich-y-rhiw

MAP 7

OL 23

N

400
200
0

7

6

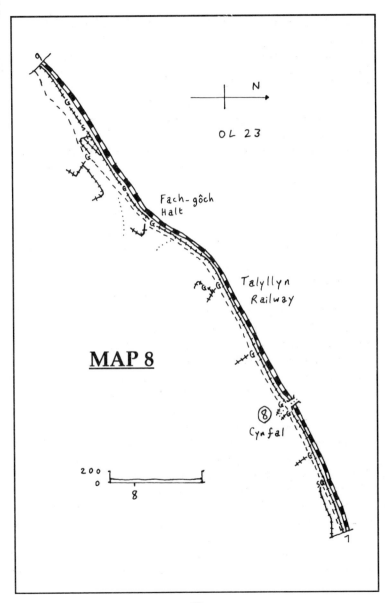

N

OL 23

Fach-gôch
Halt

Talyllyn
Railway

MAP 8

⑧
Cynfal

200
0

8

Continue to the church founded by St Cadfan in 516 to be confronted by another mysterious stone. Cadfan became known as the patron saint of warriors and led a host of saints from Brittany to Wales. Cadfan was a grandson of Emyr Llydaw, Budic, the ruler of Brittany. Perhaps he was fleeing some sort of civil war there. Tywyn became his mother church and monastic school. Cadfan went on to become the first Abbot of Bardsey. Pilgrims for Bardsey would make their way to Tywyn first, indeed St Cadfan's seems to have been a place of pilgrimage in its own right. Many people come here now to see the standing stone now kept inside the church. Dated to about 600, this is inscribed with the earliest known example of Welsh writing (earlier inscriptions were in Latin). But what does it say? Too faint to read, it has inspired controversy. The official church guide refers to 'Tengrui (or Cengrui) legal wife of Adgan, between Budd and Marciau' and 'Cun wife of Celen, loss and grief remain'. This tribute to women is admirable but an extremely rare thing for the times. The stone used to stand outside between the four small markstones which are still in the graveyard to the west of the church. It was known as Cadfan's Stone and an earlier translation of the inscription was 'The body of Cyngen is on the side between where the marks will be' and 'beneath a similar mound is extended Cadfan, sad that it should enclose the praise of the earth. May he rest without blemish'.

Would it be more likely that such a monument was erected to such notable men as St Cadfan and Cyngen, who was a son of Cadell and a contemporary of Cadfan? Cyngen succeeded his father as Prince of Powys and erected the Eliseg pillar cross near Valle Crucis Abbey, Llangollen. Cyngen's daughter, Sanan, became the wife of Maelgwn Gwynedd (but not the mother of Maelgwn's son Rhun, whose mother was Gwallwen, daughter of Afallach). Bardsey was the favoured place of burial for so many saints that it would seem strange to find the grave of the island's first abbot on the mainland. Except that Tywyn had such a strong connection with Cadfan that it would have been an appropriate last resting-place. The 1848 *Archaeologia Cambrensis* reported that Cadfan was said to have a crooked jaw. The skeleton found under this stone did have a crooked jaw.

Not far from the church, behind the Natwest Bank, is the site of St Cadfan's holy well. This was recommended to sufferers from rheumatism and arthritis. The natural chalybeate spring was enclosed in 1850 and commercial baths were opened. These closed down in the 1890s.

Tywyn gained fame in 1950 when the Talyllyn Railway was taken over by the first Railway Preservation Society in the world. Take time off this walk for a ride behind a steam engine up to Nant Gwernol and back (a round trip of 14½ miles). Learn about the history of the line that inspired the Rev. William Awdrey's railway books by visiting the museum at the Wharf Station. Telephone 01654 710472 for timetable information.

Tywyn was also the home of Marconi when he pioneered the development of radio. For almost 10 years, the main receiving station for messages from America was at Tywyn. The radio operator at Tywyn came here when he lost the toss of a coin to decide who should be the radio operator on the ill-fated Titanic.

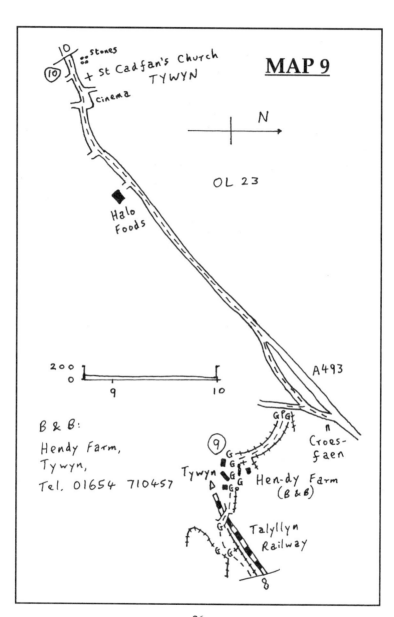

MAP 9

stones

+ St Cadfan's Church
TYWYN

cinema

N

OL 23

Halo
Foods

200
0
9   10

A493

B & B:
Hendy Farm,
Tywyn,
Tel. 01654 710457

GPG

⑨ G
        G
Tywyn ⚑ G   ⚑
        ▷ ■ Gp

Croes-
faen

Hen-dy Farm
(B & B)

G
        Talyllyn
        Railway
G G×
        8

<u>MAP 10</u>

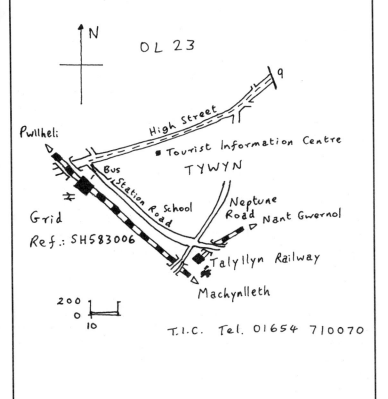

OL 23

Tywyn – Llwyngwril

Leave Tywyn by way of Sandiland. A small mansion here became a Headquarters for the RAF Regiment between 1939 and 1945. The Joint Services Mountain Training Centre remained operational here until the 1990s. The marshland was drained and turned into a small airfield. This was part of No 70 (Training) Group Farnborough and the personnel consisted of approximately 430 RAF plus 100 WAAF and No 4 RAF Regiment AA with Bofors guns. Hurricane, Mantmet and Vengeance aircraft were based here, engaged in towing duties for targets which the Royal Artillery at nearby Tonfanau could practise shooting down.

The tidal lake known as The Broadwater (there doesn't seem to be a Welsh name) has the Afon Dysynni flowing through it to the sea. This is an excellent spot for birdwatching. Look out for oystercatcher, redshank, dunlin and other waders, as well as merganser, shelduck, large gull, roost, mallard and (in winter) wigeon. Cormorants fly overhead between the sea and Craig-yr-Aderyn (Birds' Rock), while you may also see lapwing, skylark and meadow pipit.

Llanegryn's attractive church was originally dedicated to its founder, St Egryn. He is usually dated to the seventh century, but a reference to him having been a pupil of St Illtud would make him a century older. The present building was built in the 13th century by Cistercians from Cymmer Abbey, near Dolgellau. They dedicated it to St Mary the Virgin. The intricately carved rood loft and screen probably found their way here from Cymmer Abbey at the Dissolution.

Gwastad Meirionydd (mile 18) is where strange 'fairy lights' have been seen. Perhaps they are the same as were reported in 1905 near Capel Bethel, Llanfair (between miles 52 and 53) during the Mary Jones Revival.

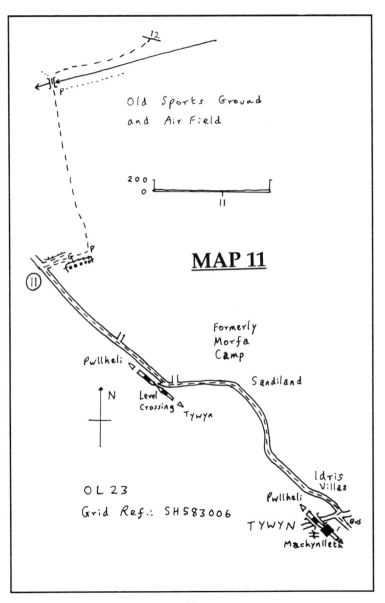

Old Sports Ground and Air Field

200
0

<u>MAP 11</u>

Formerly Morfa Camp

Pwllheli

N

Level Crossing

Tywyn

Sandiland

Idris Villas

Pwllheli

OL 23
Grid Ref.: SH583006

TYWYN

Bus

Machynlleth

29

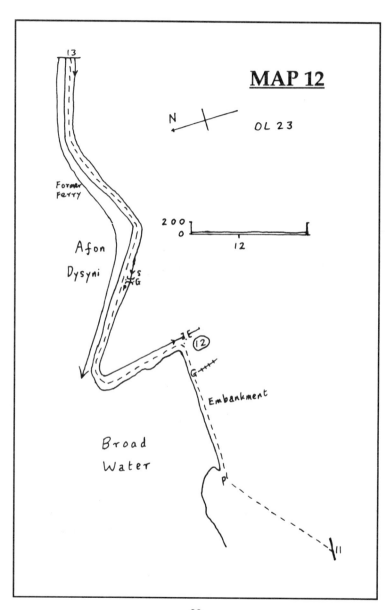

MAP 12

N

OL 23

13

Former
Ferry

Afon

Dysyni

S
P G

200
0

12

E
(12)

G

Embankment

Broad

Water

P

11

30

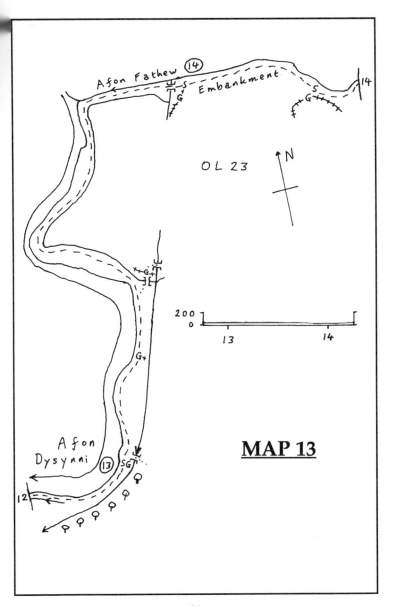

Afon Fathew ⑭

S Embankment

G

S

G

14

OL 23

N

200
0

13

14

G

G

Afon
Dysynni

⑬ SG

12

MAP 13

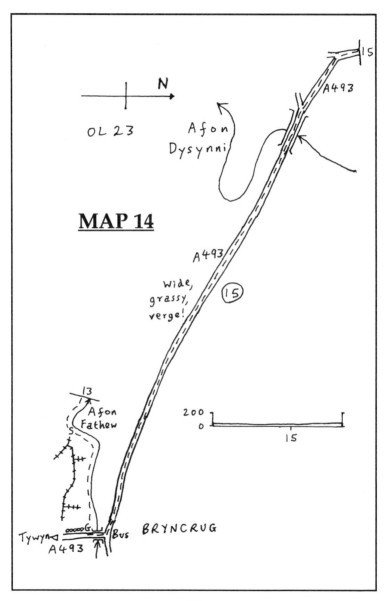

N

OL 23

Afon
Dysynni

<u>MAP 14</u>

A493

Wide,
grassy,
verge!

⑮

A493

⑮

13

Afon
Fathew

S

200
0

⑮

Tywyn◁——G:
A493

Bus

BRYNCRUG

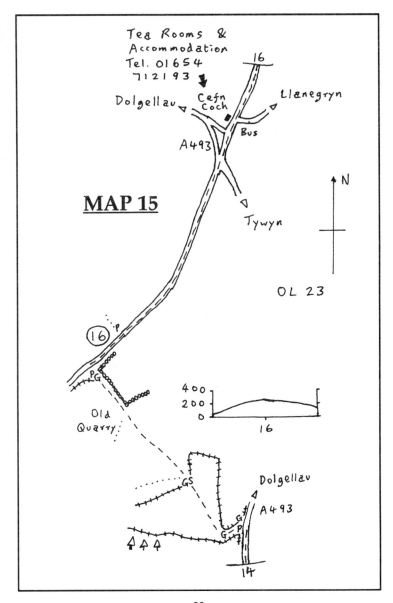

Tea Rooms &
Accommodation
Tel. 01654
712193

Dolgellau

Cefn
Coch

16

Llanegryn

Bus

A493

MAP 15

N

Tywyn

OL 23

16   P

Old
Quarry

P G

400
200
0

16

GS

Dolgellau

A493

G
G
G P

14

33

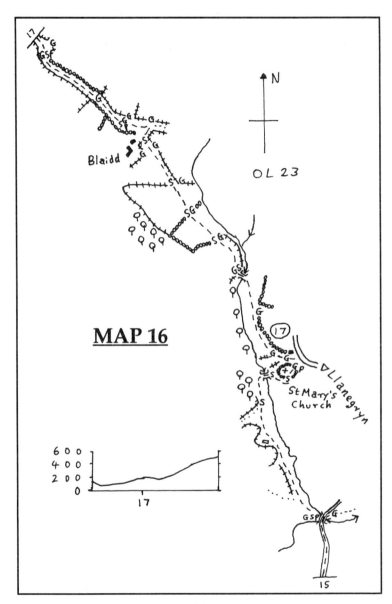

MAP 16

Blaidd

N

OL 23

17

Llanegryn

St Mary's
Church

600
400
200
0

17

GSP ← G

15

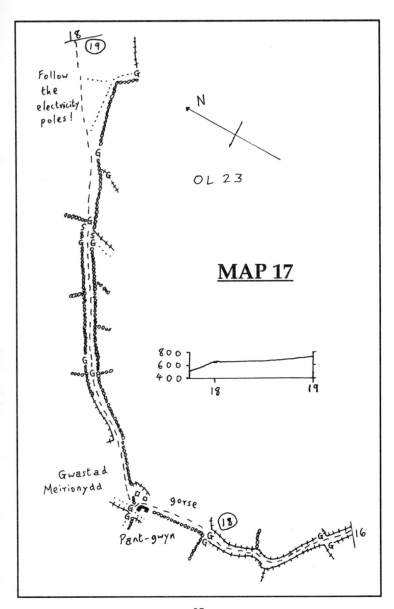

Follow the electricity poles!

N

OL 23

MAP 17

Gwastad Meirionydd

gorse

Pant-gwyn

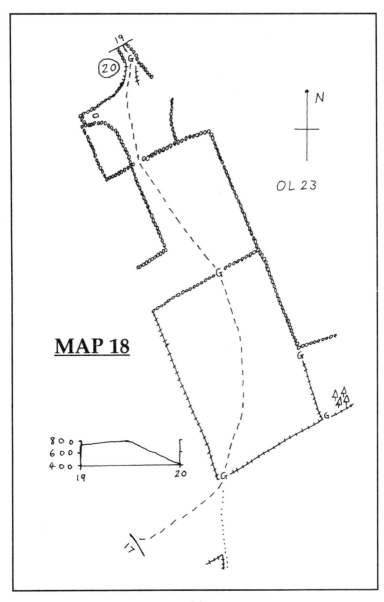

N

OL 23

MAP 18

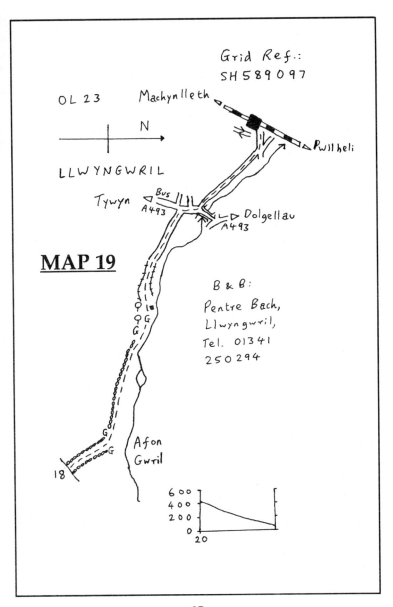

Grid Ref.:
SH 589 097

OL 23

Machynlleth

N

Pwllheli

LLWYNGWRIL

Tywyn

Bus

A493

Dolgellau

A493

MAP 19

B & B:
Pentre Bach,
Llwyngwril,
Tel. 01341
250294

G

G

G

Afon
Gwril

G

18

6 0 0
4 0 0
2 0 0
0
20

Llwyngwril – Barmouth

Follow the prehistoric track above Llwyngwril to pass several standing stones and to come close to the Grave of the King (Bedd y Brenin). This cairn is at grid ref. SH634115. If you were to follow the Ffordd Ddu (Black Road) further east, it would lead past a stone circle and more standing stones near the scenic lakes known as Llynnau Cregennen. In my book on *The Spirit Paths of Wales*, I study this route in detail as a ley or spirit path linking Llwyngwril and Dolgellau. Its angle of 60 degrees suggests the influence of moonrise in its northerly minor standstill. It is also only four degrees off the Beltane (early May) sunrise line. Most interesting is a rare example of a Welsh stone row (they are more common on Dartmoor) near mile 23.

The spirit certainly seems to move people in this area. Cyfannedd-fawr (mile 24) was where Quakers used to meet. They suffered persecution here in the 17th century. That's what happens when you seek direct personal communion with God and, dispensing with outer creeds, rites and church hierarchies, listen to the 'Inner Light'. Refusing to swear an oath of any sort, the Quakers fell foul of the Oath of Allegiance to Charles II at the Restoration in 1660 and were treated as traitors. They were forced to emigrate to America. Find out more in the Quaker Heritage Centre above the Snowdonia National Park Visitor Centre in the centre of Dolgellau. Please do cheat between miles 26 and 27 and take a ride on the narrow-gauge Fairbourne Railway between its terminus near Fairbourne's station on the Cambrian Coast Line and the railway halt with the longest name in the world – no it's not Llanfairpwllgwyngyllgogerych-wendrobwyllllantysiliogogogoch, it's Gorsafawddacha'idraig-ddanheddogleddollônpenrhynareurdraethceredigion   (The Mawddach station with its dragon's teeth on North Penrhyn Drive by the golden sands of Cardigan Bay – dragon's teeth are the World War II tank traps).

Barmouth Bridge is the jewel in the Cambrian Coast Line's crown. Luckily, for a small toll, pedestrians may also walk across it. Hundreds of timber piles support the railway across the sand of the estuary. A steel revolving section spans the navigable channel at the Barmouth end. It's ages since it has been swung open. There can be few finer sights than the view up the Mawddach with Cadair Idris in the background, although the northern shore is attractive too. The Cambrian Way also uses the path across Barmouth Bridge on its 274 mile journey between Cardiff and Conwy.

The funfair and fleshpots of Barmouth may come as a shock to the system after days spent walking in the hills. This is the major resort on the Cambrian Coast. It stands at the foot of Dinas Oleu (Fortress of Light). When I once spent a week fasting at the summit of Cadair Idris, I dowsed the most important ley or spirit path going through the summit of that powerful peak. The ley went towards Dinas Oleu. The grave of a Frenchman who migrated to Barmouth is to be found on this sacred spot. August Guyard was a friend of both Victor Hugo and John Ruskin. Ruskin's Guild of St George was presented with property here in 1875 by Mrs Talbot. The Frenchman was a tenant of one of the houses. Mrs Talbot also gave Dinas Oleu to the fledgling National Trust in 1895. The harbour offers boat trips, including the ferry service to the Porth Penrhyn terminus of the Fairbourne Railway. There is an interesting Life Boat Museum. When casting your eye over the sea, be prepared for a surprise! On 2 March, 1975, six local schoolgirls saw 'Barmy, the Mawddach Monster'. It had a long neck, a square face, a long tail, a flipper at its back and black, patchy skin. Similar sightings have been recorded over the years. Was this mystery solved on 23 September, 1989, when the world's largest sea turtle, weighing 2016 lbs and almost nine feet long, was washed ashore at Harlech? It died after becoming entangled in whelk fishing lines. The turtle is now on display in the National Museum of Wales.

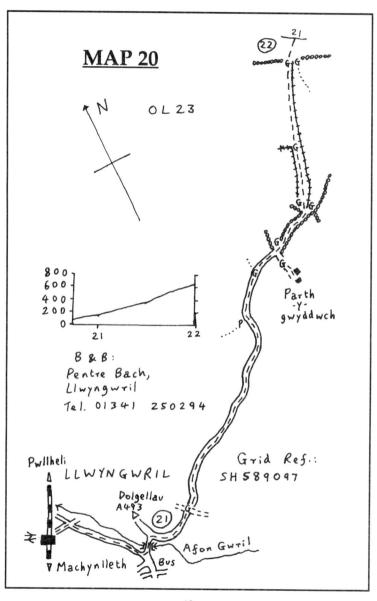

MAP 20

N

OL 23

㉒ 21

G G

G

G G

G

G

Parth -y- gwyddwch

P

800
600
400
200

21   22

B & B :
Pentre Bach,
Llwyngwril
Tel. 01341 250294

Grid Ref.:
SH 589097

Pwllheli
LLWYNGWRIL

Dolgellau
A493

㉑

G

Afon Gwril

Machynlleth   Bus

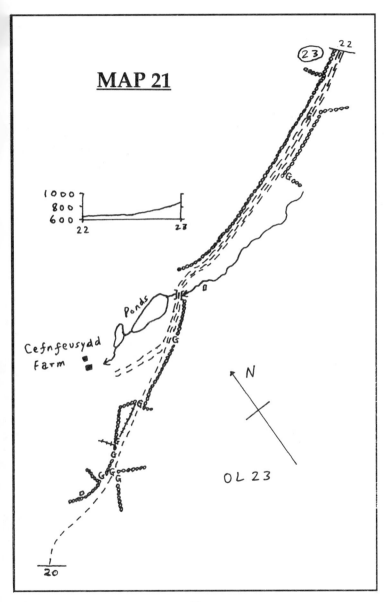

MAP 21

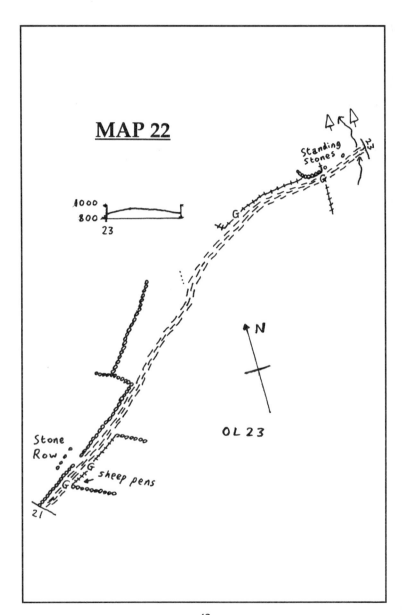

MAP 22

Standing Stones

1000
800
23

G

G

N

OL 23

Stone Row

G sheep pens

G

21

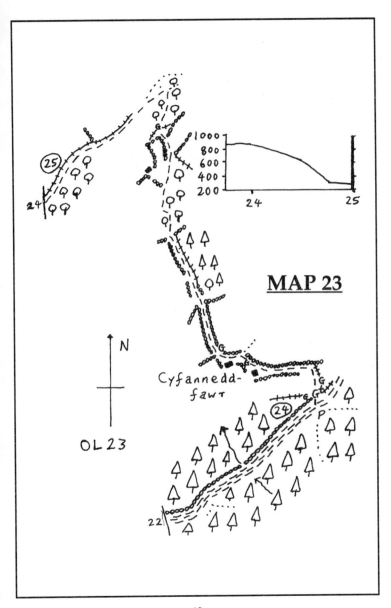

MAP 23

Cyfanedd-fawr

N

OL 23

43

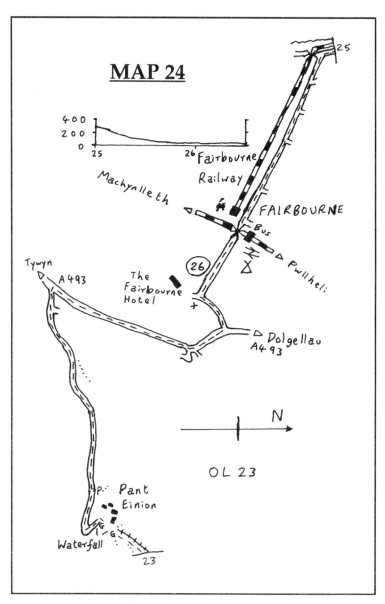

MAP 24

400
200
0

25   26 Fairbourne
                        Railway

Machynlleth

FAIRBOURNE

Bus

Pwllheli

Tywyn

A 493

The
Fairbourne
Hotel

26

Dolgellau
A 493

N

OL 23

Pant
Einion

P.

G

Waterfall

23

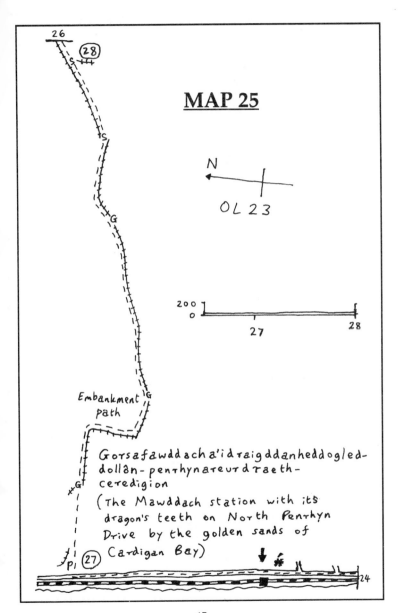

MAP 25

N

OL 23

200
0

27   28

Embankment
path

Gorsafawddacha'idraigddanheddogled-
dollân-penrhynareurdraeth-
ceredigion

(The Mawddach station with its
dragon's teeth on North Penrhyn
Drive by the golden sands of
Cardigan Bay)

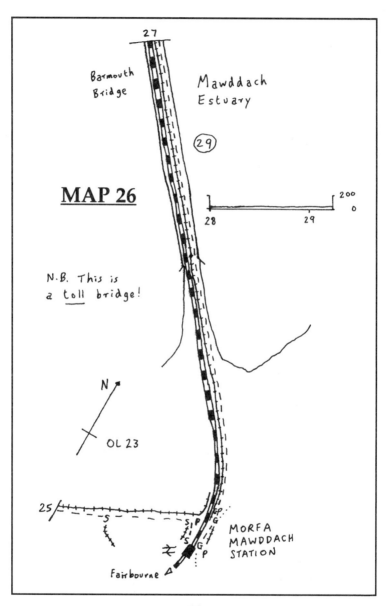

27

Barmouth
Bridge

Mawddach
Estuary

(29)

MAP 26

200
0
28   29

N.B. This is
a toll bridge!

N

OL 23

25

MORFA
MAWDDACH
STATION

S
S   I   P
G
G   P
P

Fairbourne

MAP 27

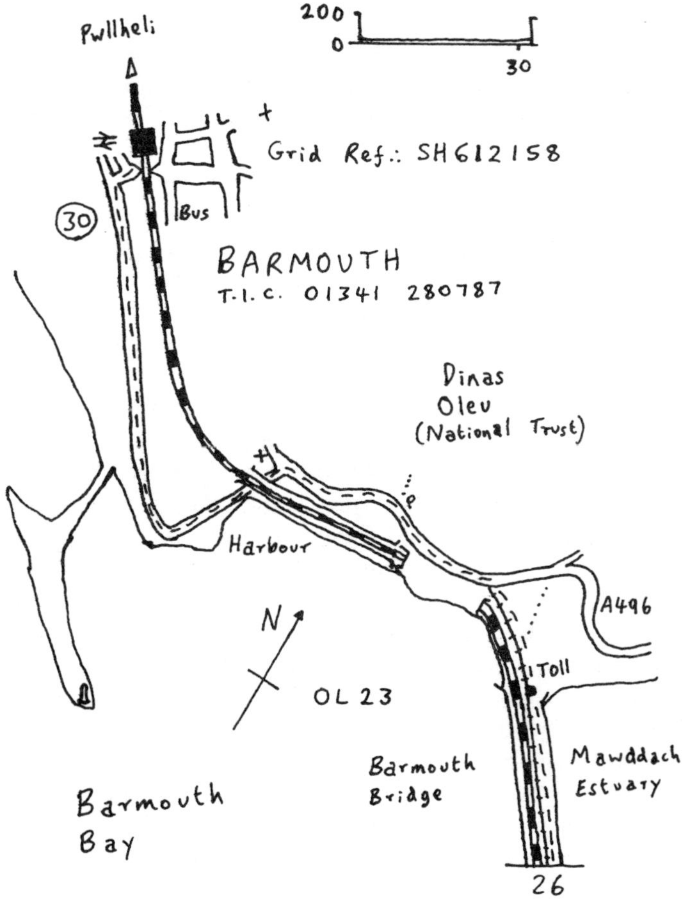

Pwllheli

200
0
30

Grid Ref.: SH 612 158

Bus

BARMOUTH
T.I.C. 01341 280787

Dinas
Oleu
(National Trust)

Harbour

N

OL 23

A496

Toll

Barmouth
Bridge

Mawddach
Estuary

Barmouth
Bay

26

Barmouth – Talybont

St John's Church, Barmouth, should have had its foundation stone laid by Queen Victoria in 1889. Her daughter Princess Beatrice was sent instead as the Non-Conformists were outraged by the continuing establishment of the Church in Wales and the tithes which they had to pay.

You may be daunted by the steep climb from Barmouth, but having made it you'll find it hard to leave this rugged, beautiful wilderness. Bwlch y Llan was the scene of a tragedy on 26/27 December 1943 when an Avro Anson attached to 9 Observers Advance Flying Unit flew into the hill in low cloud. The aircraft was on a routine navigation exercise and was returning to its base at nearby RAF Llandwrog. All four of the crew were killed.

Only a few stones are left of Cerrig Arthur stone circle (mile 33). The axis of the ring, which has a radius of nearly 10 megalithic yards, points south-south-east to where the extreme southerly rising of the moon would have taken place in 1700 BC.

The mortally-wounded King Arthur was most probably taken by boat from the Mawddach estuary after the Battle of Camlan in 537. Many prehistoric monuments are named after Arthur, of course. The prospect of many Arthurs – of Arthur as a title – must also be considered. It does so happen that about one mile north-east of Cerrig Arthur stone circle at grid ref. SH644199 (approx.), where the Ordnance Survey Outdoor Leisure 23 map marks 'Cerrig y Cledd' is a boulder which bears the magical imprint of an ancient British sword. A similar imprint is on a second rock lying at its foot. Two halves of a split rock? Legend has a sword being tossed at the rock after a battle and leaving its outline for eternity.

Between miles 36 and 37 are the remains of one of several stone circles in the vicinity. This one is at grid ref. SH611218. A

Start from Aberdyfi Station
(Mile 0)

Above Aberdyfi
(Miles 0-1)

*Between miles 2 & 3, near
Dyffryn Glyn-Cul*

*Croes Faen, Tywyn
(Mile 9)*

*The Markstones in the
Graveyard of St Cadfan's
Church, Tywyn (Mile 10)*

*The Cadfan Stone in
Tywyn Church
(Mile 10)*

Looking up the Dysynni Valley to Birds' Rock (Craig yr Aderyn)
from the Broadwater (Mile 12)

Looking towards Craig yr Aderyn (Birds' Rock)
and Cadair Idris from near Mile 16

The Rood Screen, Llanegryn Church
(Mile 17)

The track down to Llwyngwril
(Mile 20)

The Stone Row near Mile 23

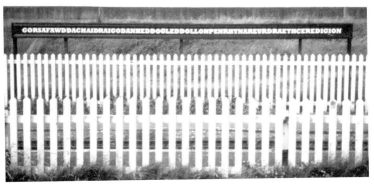

The longest station name in the world
(Mile 27)

Crossing Barmouth Bridge
(Mile 29)

Cadair Idris, Barmouth Harbour and Railway Bridge
(Near Mile 30)

Arrows mark the path above Barmouth
(Mile 31)

Overlooking Barmouth Bay from Gell Fawr
(Near Mile 31)

Cerrig Arthur Stone Circle,
with Diffwys beyond
(Miles 33-34)

A Holy Well in the foothills of
the Rhinog Mountains north of
Cerrig Arthur Stone Circle
(Mile 34)

Cors y Gedol Burial Chamber
(Approaching Mile 41)

Heading for Llanbedr
(Mile 43)

A copy of Vosper's painting,
Capel Salem (Miles 46-47)

Capel Salem
(Miles 46-47)

57

The prehistoric carved spiral stone inside St Peter's Church, Llanbedr (Mile 48)

Meini Hirion – standing stones at Llanbedr (Mile 48)

The walled path from Llanfair to Llandanwg (Mile 51)

St Tanwg's Church, Llandanwg
(Mile 51)

The Beach at Llandanwg
(Mile 51)

Capel Bethel, Llanfair, where 'Earthlights' were seen in 1905
(Miles 52-53)

Approaching Harlech and Mile 53

Harlech Castle
(Mile 55)

Harlech Castle
(Mile 55)

Harlech Castle
(Mile 55)

The Beady Eye of the Standing Stone
(Mile 58)

The Lower Ring Cairn Circle below Moel Goedog
(Miles 58-59)

Bryn Cader Faner
(Miles 61-62)

Approaching Mile 62 after
Bryn Cader Faner

Cross this stream at Mile 62

Cross this stile at Mile 62
(After Bryn Cader Faner)

Descending to Mile 63 and
Nant Pasgan-Bach

Llyn Tecwyn Isaf
(Mile 65)

Dutch psychologist, Dr H Van Der Helm-Hylkema, who regularly spends her holidays in Wales, consequently bought my walking guidebooks and subscribed to *The Ley Hunter* (magazine of leys and Earth Mysteries), saw 'a ball of white transparent light' here in 1993. Was this the same phenomenon witnessed in 1904 and 1905 during the Mary Jones religious revival? Did our prehistoric ancestors witness such lights and were they influenced into erecting stone circles by them? Does the presence of stone circles encourage the lights? Paul Devereux compares such lights to modern sightings of UFOs in his books *Earthlights* (1982) and *Earth Lights Revelation* (1989). Capel Egryn (grid ref. SH594204) was a focus of the lights in 1905, but then the chapel was where people congregated. Who would witness a light higher up (just two miles east of Capel Egryn) on a February evening? *The Daily Mirror* of 16 February 1905 did report 'a large square of light' over the top of the mountains a mile from Capel Egryn:

'It did not rest on the mountain-top, but was poised in mid-air about ten feet above. Between it and the mountain was a mass of white cloud. In the middle of the square was a bottle-shaped body, the bottom bright blue and the rest black. Out of the neck came a mass of fire of every conceivable colour. This . . . spreading on all sides, descended in a rainbow shower to the surface of the mountain. In less than a minute all was darkness.'

Earth lights and stone circles seem to correlate with faultlines. Capel Egryn is on the same Mochras Fault as Capel Bethel, Llanfair (between miles 52 and 53 of this walk). Read more about such lights when you reach there. One of the minerals found in this area is zirconium. The pyroelectrical properties of zircon seem of interest. It may produce an electrical charge when heated. Is this not, too, evidence of the living nature of Mother Earth?

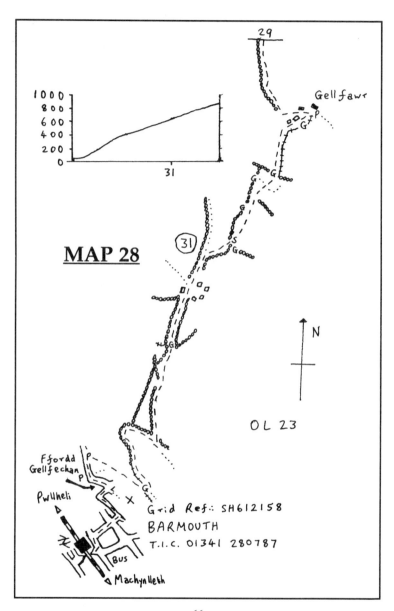

MAP 28

29

Gellfawr

G

G

G

S
G

31

G

N

OL 23

Ffordd
Gellfechan

P

P

G

Pwllheli

X

Grid Ref: SH612158
BARMOUTH
T.I.C. 01341 280787

BUS

Machynlleth

1000
800
600
400
200
0

31

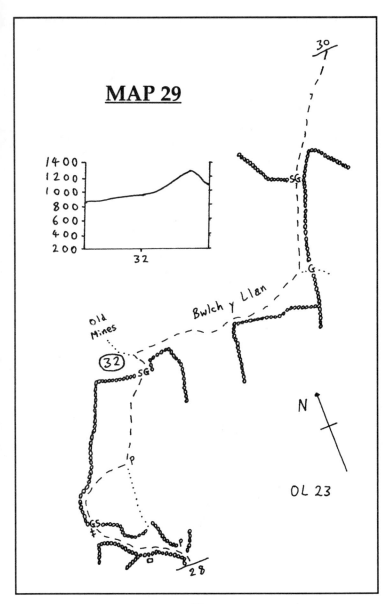

MAP 29

30

1400
1200
1000
800
600
400
200

32

SG

G

Bwlch y Llan

Old Mines

(32)

SG

P

N

OL 23

GS

28

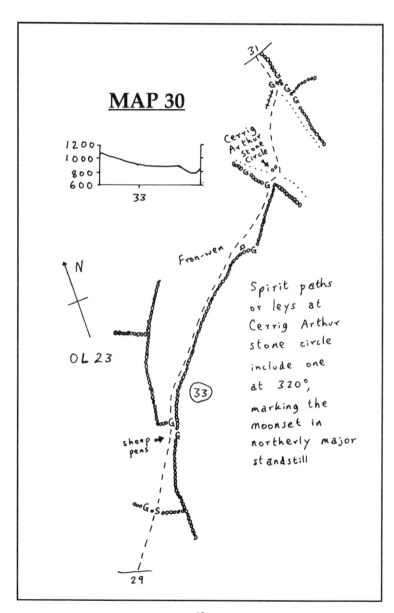

MAP 30

31

Cerrig Arthur Stone Circle

Fron-wen

N

OL 23

33

sheep pens

G•S

29

Spirit paths or leys at Cerrig Arthur stone circle include one at 320°, marking the moonset in northerly major standstill

1200
1000
800
600
33

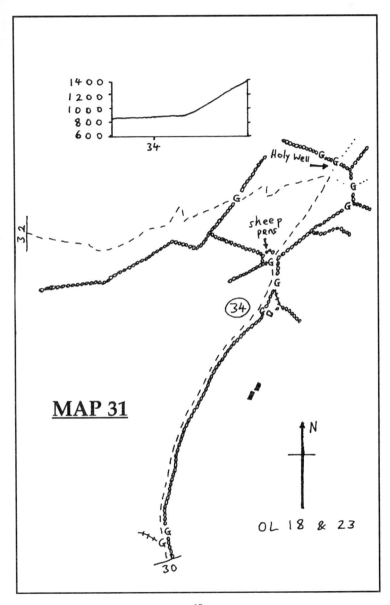

MAP 31

Holy Well

sheep pens

OL 18 & 23

N

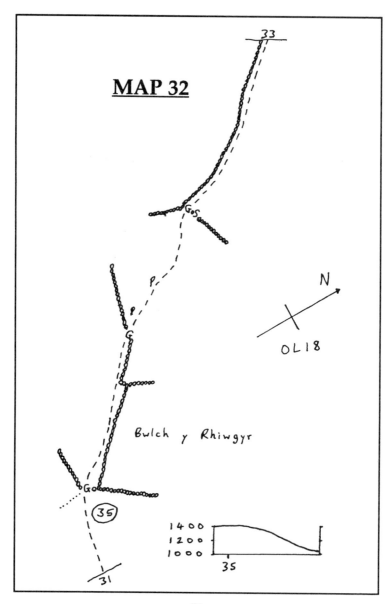

MAP 32

33

GoS

P

P

G

Bwlch y Rhiwgyr

G

(35)

N

OL18

1400
1200
1000

35

31

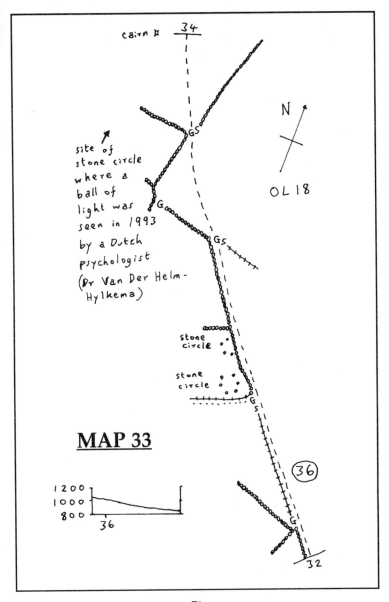

cairn ⌗ _34_

site of
stone circle
where a
ball of
light was
seen in 1993
by a Dutch
psychologist
(Dr Van Der Helm-
Hylkema)

N

OL 18

GS

G

GS

stone
circle

stone
circle

GS

MAP 33

36

G

1200
1000
800

36

32

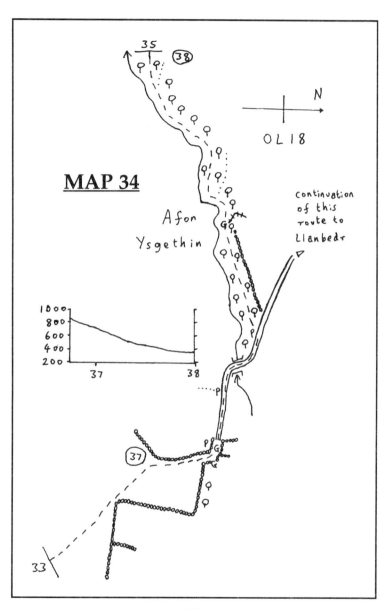

MAP 34

Afon Ysgethin

continuation of this route to Llanbedr

OL 18

N

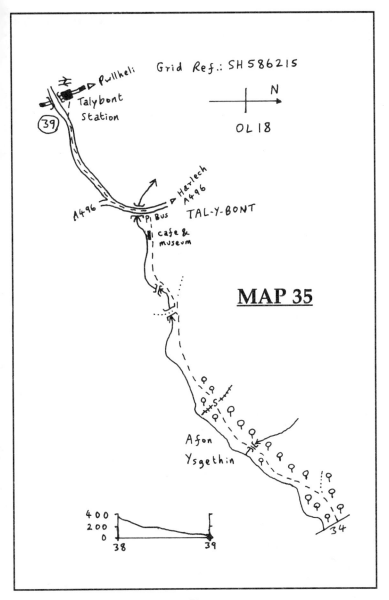

Grid Ref.: SH 586215

N

OL 18

Pwllheli

Talybont
Station

39

A496

Harlech
A496

TAL-Y-BONT

Pt Bus

cafe &
museum

MAP 35

Afon
Ysgethin

S

34

400
200
0

38   39

Talybont – Llanbedr

The Ysgethin Inn, Talybont, began life as a pandy or fulling mill in 1788. A woollen factory replaced it in 1880 and the building became an inn in the 1930s, although part of it may always have served to quench the thirsts of locals and travellers. More of this area's past can be discovered from a visit to the nearby Rural Life Museum.

Pass the cromlech or Neolithic burial chamber known as Cors y Gedol. Dating from at least 5000 years ago, probably 2000 years before the remains of huts and fields within half a mile east of it, this cromlech prompts the question have later farmers conformed to much earlier boundaries? What would the view over the sea in the west have been like when Cors y Gedol was erected? Sarn Badrig extends under the waves towards Ireland. This causeway can still be identified at low tide. Was it a legendary wall of Cantre'r Gwaelod? Geologists have examined the Sarn and conclude that it is a product of the last Ice Age – natural, not man-made. Around 5000 BC or 4000 BC (and some would date Cors y Gedol to 4000 BC) this natural barrier would have protected a fertile plain to its south from the sea to its north. Peninsulas and off-shore islands at the ends of peninsulas also had great religious importance to our ancestors. Neolithic man could well have witnessed the loss of this land and remembered it in legends that have come down to us. Any loss of land around AD 500 (as at Aberdyfi) would have involved a mere fragment of the land known to our Stone Age ancestors.

Capel Salem (between miles 46 and 47) is an isolated Baptist chapel that became famous, and notorious, when Sydney Curnow Vosper painted a picture in it in 1908. Siân Owen, an old lady in a shawl, is depicted holding her Bible or hymn book inside the chapel. Admirers of the painting soon reported seeing the outline of the devil in her shawl. If you have difficulty seeing it, that proves your own purity! The artist never confirmed being conscious of it. Siân actually wore a simpler shawl and had borrowed this one for the painting. None of the ladies featured in the painting actually owned a hat yet Vosper used his artistic licence to include them. An old, out-of-fashion, hat was actually borrowed from the grandmother of Rev. Evan Rowlands and shared around for the painting. The virtues of Non-Conformism were portrayed just four years after the great revival (and mysterious lights) of 1904. Did the artist also intend to portray Welsh hypocrisy? Siân lived a further 19 years with people pointing to the devil in her shawl. She died aged 90 and was buried at Llanfair, not here. Her tombstone has the telling words 'I am afflicted above measure: give me life, O Lord, according to Thy Word'.

The painting in Capel Salem is a copy. The original is in the Lady Lever Art Gallery in Port Sunlight. Lord Leverhulme bought it in 1909 for one hundred guineas and presented copies to people who bought lots of his Sunlight soap. It has featured as the cover of calendars and postcards of Vosper's painting are available. A second, half-size, original of this scene was painted by Vosper for his brother-in-law and has been inherited by a Worcester lady.

Divert from this route at Llanbedr to visit St Peter's Church. This houses a stone carved with a spiral in either the Neolithic or Bronze Age. It came from the Irishmen's huts above Dyffryn Ardudwy and is probably an aid to meditation in order to enter a state of trance. From the 1850s to the early 1900s it was kept between the two standing stones known as Meini Hirion about 200 yards west of the church. One of these stones stands an impressive 10 feet high, dwarfing its six feet six inches neighbour.

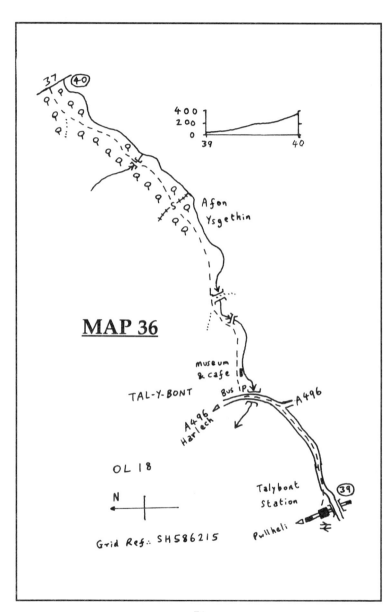

37 (40)

400
200
0
39   40

Afon
Ysgethin

MAP 36

museum
& cafe

TAL-Y-BONT   Bus IP   A496

A496
Harlech

OL 18

N

Talybont
Station   39

Pwllheli

Grid Ref: SH586215

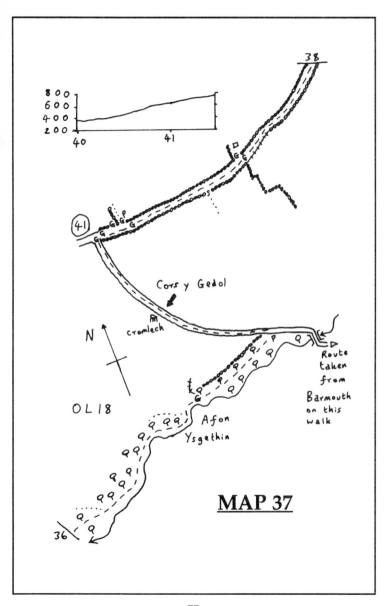

38

800
600
400
200
40   41

41

Cors y Gedol

cromlech

N

OL 18

Route
taken
from
Barmouth
on this
walk

Afon
Ysgethin

MAP 37

36

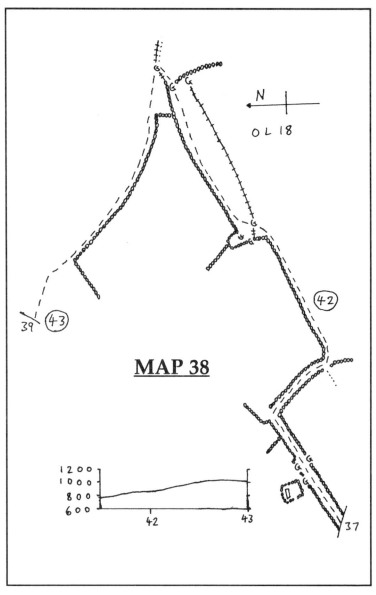

N

OL 18

(42)

39 (43)

MAP 38

1 2 0 0
1 0 0 0
8 0 0
6 0 0

42   43

37

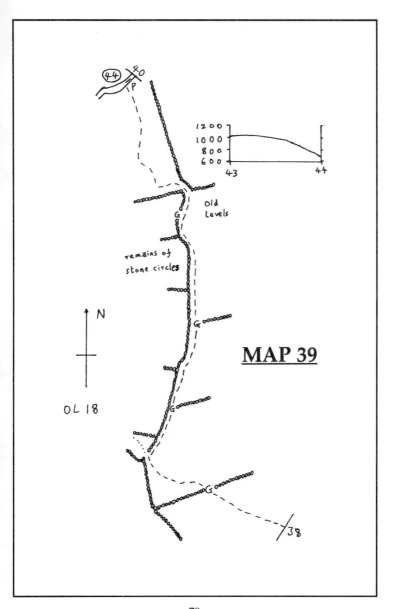

(44) 40

P

1200
1000
800
600

43   44

Old
Levels

G

remains of
stone circles

↑ N

G

MAP 39

G

OL 18

G

G

/38

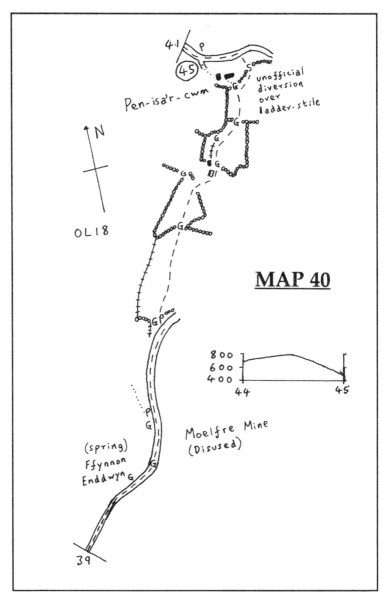

41

P

(45)

Pen-isa'r-cwm

unofficial
diversion
over
ladder-stile

G

G

G

G

↑N

OL18

G

G

G

MAP 40

GP

800
600
400

44   45

P

G

Moelfre Mine
(Disused)

(spring)
Ffynnon
Enddwyn G

G

39

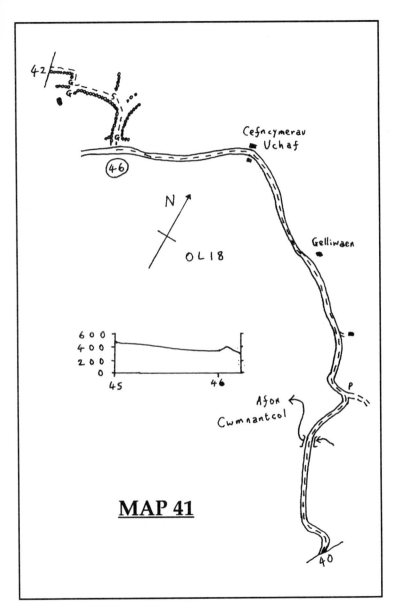

42

Cefncymerau
Uchaf

46

N

OL18

Gelliwaen

P

600
400
200
0
45   46

Afon
Cwmnantcol

MAP 41

40

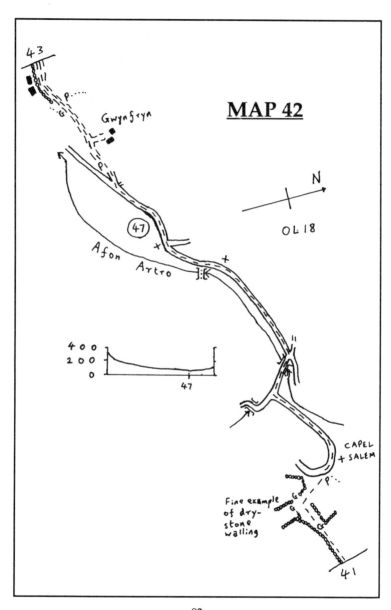

MAP 42

N

OL 18

43

Gwynfryn

47

Afon Artro

400
200
0

47

CAPEL
+ SALEM

Fine example
of dry-
stone
walling

41

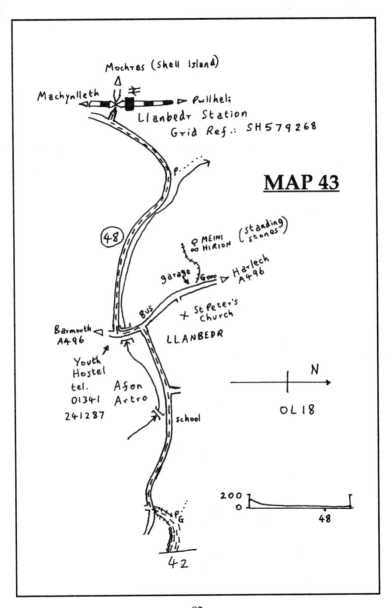

Mochras (Shell Island)

Machynlleth ◁ ▷ Pwllheli

Llanbedr Station
Grid Ref.: SH 579 268

MAP 43

48

MEINI (standing stones)
HIRION

garage ▷ Harlech A496

Bus ✝ St Peter's Church

Barmouth A496 ◁ LLANBEDR

Youth Hostel tel. 01341 241287

Afon Artro

school

N

OL 18

200
0   48

P G

42

83

Llanbedr – Harlech

The Slate Caverns at Old Llanfair Quarry (mile 50) are worth diverting to, especially on a hot day when you'll welcome the reduction in temperature to a fairly constant 50 degrees. Be warned, put on extra clothes! Slate was quarried here from 1877 to 1906, meeting the demand for roofing slates created by the Industrial Revolution. Small ships were able to dock at nearby Pensarn and export slate to Hamburg. As roofing tiles replaced slate, demand declined, production costs rose and the quarries closed.

Descend to the beach at Llandanwg to see the ancient 'church on the sands'. This is dedicated to St Tanwg and may well date from AD 435 (and some English people think Christianity came to Britain with St Augustine in 597!). During the Middle Ages, when the dead who could afford it were taken for burial on Bardsey Island, this church was 'a Chapell of Rest for corpses to be transported to yt fam'd Repository at Bardsey Island'. A pillar stone lying by the altar dates from the fifth century and may have come from the Wicklow Hills in Ireland. A gravestone for Equester (a knight?) dates from the fifth or sixth centuries, while another gravestone bears a cross which dates it to the eighth century. St Tanwg may have been related to St Cadfan and was one of the saints who accompanied him in 516. On Sundays in July and August you can combine this walk with a family service (come straight from the beach!) at 3.30 pm, while there is also a service at 6.30 pm on the third Sunday of every month (telephone 01341 247207 to confirm the times of services).

St Mary's Church, Llanfair, is said to mark where the mother of Jesus actually came (and she is said to have bathed in nearby Hafod-y-Llyn). The west of Britain and its mineral wealth did attract traders from the Middle East thousands of years ago. Legend does credit Mary with a British mother, St Ann. *The Marian Conspiracy* by Graham Phillips (2000) makes interesting reading, linking Mary with Gwynedd.

Llanfair's Capel Bethel is situated precisely on the Mochras Fault and the mysterious Earth Lights seen at 9.15 pm on 25 March 1905 'ascending from one side of the chapel, the side which is in a field' emerged directly from the faultline. 'Balls of light, deep red' were observed. Seen in 1905 these were associated with the religious revival. Mary Jones told *The Daily Mail* she thought they were 'Heaven-sent', although she admitted to *The Guardian* 'Well, they don't go with me as much as I should like'. Modern observers would probably detail abductions by aliens. Whatever the answer, this is a place to look out for strange lights.

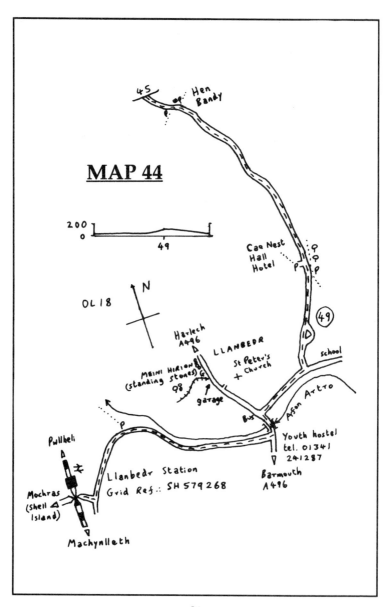

MAP 44

45

Hen Bandy

200
0

49

OL 18

N

Cae Nest
Hall
Hotel

P

49

Harlech
A496

LLANBEDR

St Peter's
+ Church

school

Meini Hirion
(standing stones)

98

garage

Afon Artro

Bus

Youth hostel
tel. 01341
241287

Pwllheli

P

Barmouth
A496

Mochras
(Shell
Island)

Llanbedr Station
Grid Ref.: SH 579 268

Machynlleth

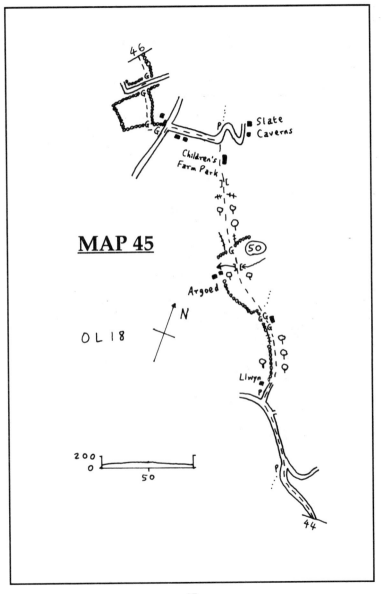

MAP 45

46

Slate
Caverns

Children's
Farm Park

50

Argoed

N

OL 18

Llwyn

200
0
50

44

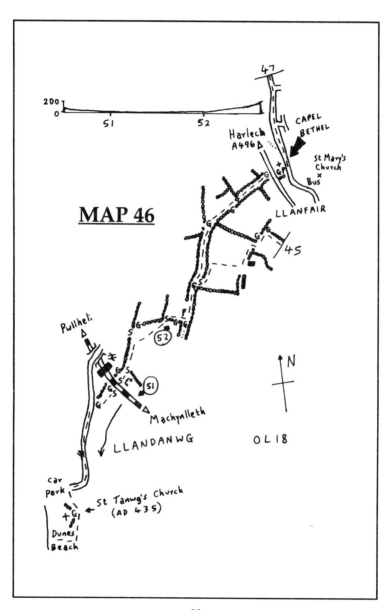

MAP 46

47

CAPEL BETHEL

Harlech A496

St Mary's Church

Bus

LLANFAIR

45

Pwllheli

52

51

Machynlleth

LLANDANWG

OL18

N

car park

St Tanwg's Church (AD 435)

Dunes Beach

200
0
51   52

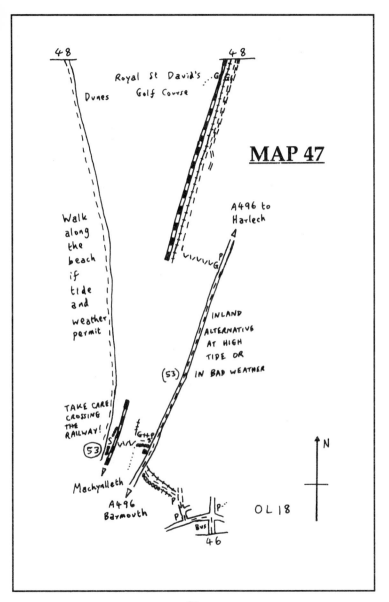

48

48

Royal St David's G G|

Golf Course

Dunes

MAP 47

A496 to
Harlech

Walk
along
the
beach
if
tide
and
weather
permit

INLAND
ALTERNATIVE
AT HIGH
TIDE OR
IN BAD WEATHER

(53)

TAKE CARE!
CROSSING
THE
RAILWAY!

G+P

(53) S

N

Machynlleth

A496
Barmouth

P

P

P

OL 18

Bus

46

GRADIENT PROFILE FOR BEACH
ROUTE:

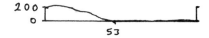

GRADIENT PROFILE FOR INLAND
ALTERNATIVE:

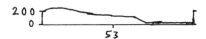

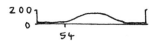

Whether walking along the beach or taking the inland alternative route to Harlech, your eyes will be drawn to its magnificent castle. Before visiting this official World Heritage Site, which is in the care of Cadw (Heritage in Wales), look for the statue on its left-hand side as you face the main entrance of the castle and look towards the sea. Known as 'The Two Kings', this sculpture shows Bendigeidfran bearing the body of his nephew Gwern and is a symbol of the sorrowful burden endured by love.

Harlech Castle is set on Tŵr Branwen, or Branwen's Tower. Perhaps its close association with a goddess led to Robert Graves liking it so much. This author did live at Harlech for a while and when he settled on a Majorcan mountainside, where he wrote *The White Goddess*, he did so because the view reminded him of Harlech. Branwen (White Crow or White Bosom) was the daughter of Llŷr whose story forms the second of the Four Branches of the Mabinogi.

One afternoon as Bendigeidfran (Bran the Blessed), the brother of Branwen, was sitting on a rock at Harlech, where he held a court, he spotted 13 ships coming from the south of Ireland. Branwen was eventually married to Matholwch, King of Ireland, but suffered abuse and injustice there. This stemmed from the way her half-brother Efnisien had insulted Matholwch by maiming his horses. Bran tried to repair the damage by giving the Irish king the magical Cauldron of Rebirth that would restore life to any slain warrior, although leaving him dumb.

When a starling carried a message from Branwen to Bran detailing the dishonour inflicted upon her, the British invaded Ireland. Bran waded across as no ship could contain him and the Irish Sea was shallower and narrower in those days. This resulted in a peace conference where the Irish intended treachery but Efnisien foiled their ruse. It was then agreed that Gwern, Branwen's son, should be King of Ireland. Efnisien threw the boy into the fire, however, and in the subsequent fight the Cauldron of Rebirth was granting numerical superiority to the Irish. Efnisien, pretending to be one of the Irish dead, was thrown into the cauldron where he stretched himself and burst its sides, dying in the process. Seven survivors returned to Britain, carrying Bran's severed head. This spent seven years at Harlech, being feasted and serenaded by the Birds of Rhiannon. Bran's head was later buried under the Tower of London, although Arthur unwisely dug it up later.

Built to consolidate Edward I's conquest of Wales in 1283, the castle was designed to be defended by only 30 men. The sea used to lap the rock on which it stood, allowing for supplies to be brought by boat to the foot of the castle. Owain Glyndŵr succeeded in starving the garrison into submission when he cut off this life-line in 1404. He went on to hold a parliament here in 1405. The fortunes of war led to his own family being starved into surrender at Harlech in 1408. Henry IV took Margaret, Glyndŵr's wife, and two of their daughters prisoner.

Another long siege in the Wars of the Roses, when Sir Dafydd ap Ieuan sheltered the future Henry VII against the Yorkist army, inspired the song 'Men of Harlech'. Harlech was also the last castle to submit in the Civil War between Charles I and Cromwell. Allow time to climb the 143 steps to the top of the left inner turret of the gatehouse and note how the sand dunes have spread since the 13th century.

Graves recognised Harlech as a likely place for a sacred alder-grove.

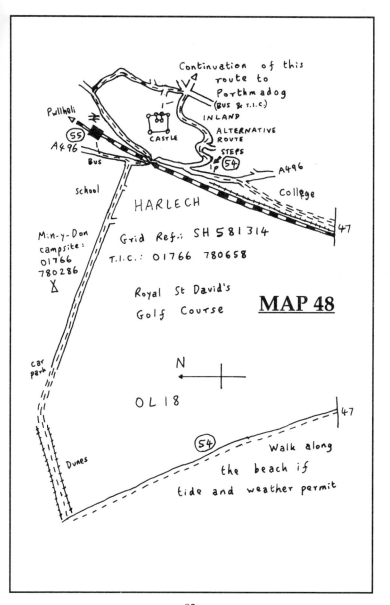

Continuation of this route to Porthmadog
(BUS & T.I.C.)

INLAND ALTERNATIVE ROUTE

STEPS

54

Pwllheli

55

A496

Bus

CASTLE

A496

College

school

HARLECH

47

Min-y-Don campsite: 01766 780286

Grid Ref.: SH 581 314

T.I.C.: 01766 780658

Royal St David's Golf Course

MAP 48

car park

N

OL 18

47

Dunes

54

Walk along the beach if tide and weather permit

Harlech – Llandecwyn

Anyone familiar with Terence Meaden's book *The Secrets of the Avebury Stones* (1999) will recognise faces in ancient standing stones. They also appear in dreams if you sleep beside them, in my experience. This walk takes you above Harlech to join what appears to be more than a prehistoric track. It is lined by standing stones, leads to stone circles (or cairn circles) and would seem to be an ancient ceremonial way. This may be linked with the line of the summer solstice sunrise (50 degrees).

Look especially at the faces of the stones on either side of the road at the point where you fork right off the metalled road to follow the signposted path (mile 58). The stones guide you to a pair of circles, of which the path affords a fine view of the lower ring. Circles often come in pairs, like wedding rings. Perhaps they are contemporary, or maybe a second circle reflects a slight movement in the sacred site. Perhaps they represent the hands of the Goddess, with the stones sticking out of the ground like her fingers. Within the circle is a cauldron which contains spirit, particularly at special times such as the summer solstice. Heaven and earth meet and mate here and the resulting spirit goes forth along leys or spirit paths to fertilise the land. Two circles would therefore represent both hands of the Goddess. These are known as ring cairns and have been dated to between 1700 and 1400 BC.

Bryn Cader Faner (between miles 61 and 62) has the most beautiful, jagged, silhouette of any Bronze Age monument in Britain. It is a cairn circle, being more of a gravemound than a ceremonial circle. Such places are full of mystery. Understanding may have been lost, but a sense of awe and respect remain. How many such circles have we passed on this walk?

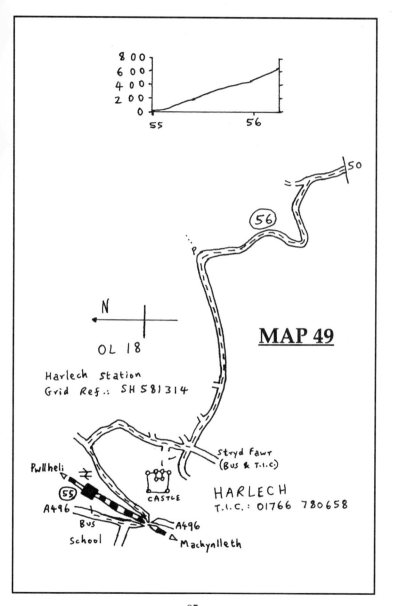

MAP 49

N

OL 18

Harlech station
Grid Ref.: SH 581314

Stryd Fawr
(Bus & T.I.C.)

Pwllheli

55

A496

Bus

School

A496

Machynlleth

CASTLE

HARLECH
T.I.C.: 01766 780658

56

50

P

MAP 50

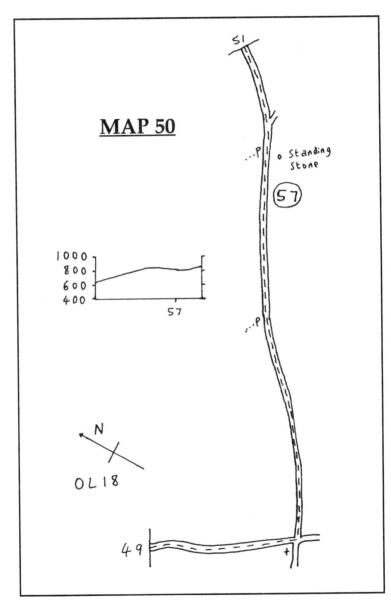

51

...P ○ Standing
           Stone

(57)

1000
800
600
400
                    57

N

OL18

49   +

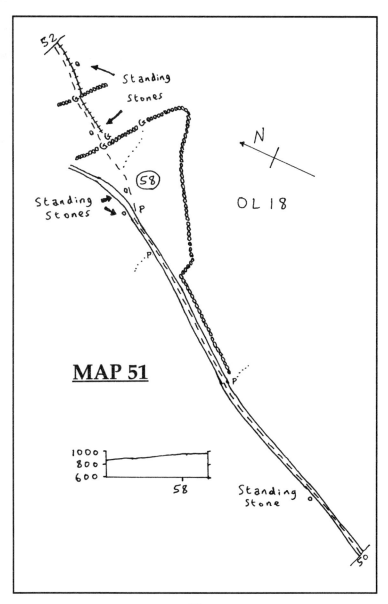

52

Standing Stones

Standing Stones

(58)

P

P

Standing Stones

P

N

OL 18

MAP 51

1000
800
600

58

Standing Stone

50

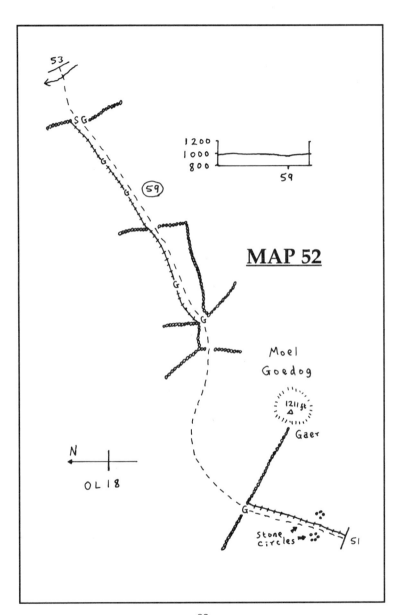

53

S G

G

(59)

1200
1000
800   59

G

MAP 52

G

G

Moel
Goedog

1211ft
△

Gaer

N

OL 18

G

Stone
Circles

51

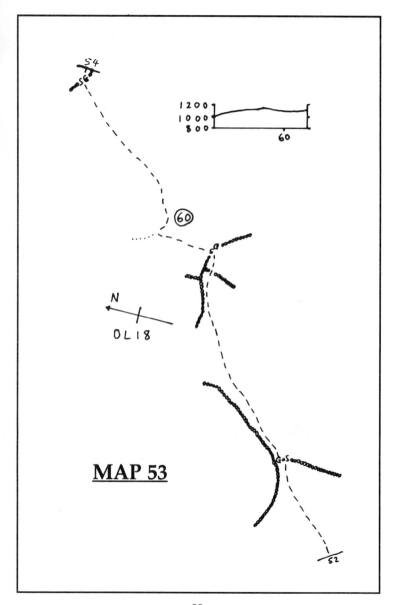

MAP 53

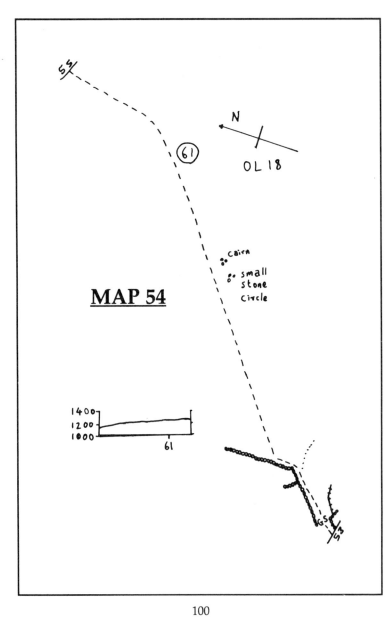

MAP 54

N

OL 18

54

61

Cairn

small
stone
Circle

1400
1200
1000

61

GS

53

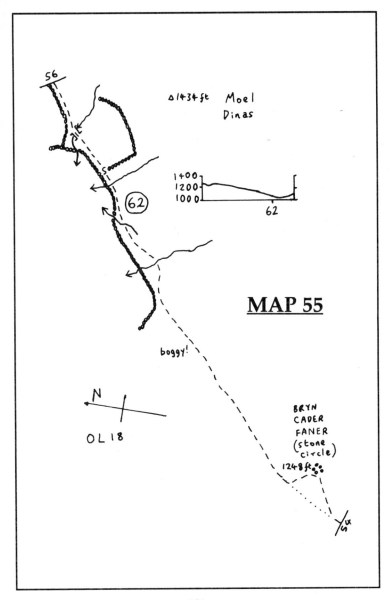

56

△1434 ft Moel
Dinas

1400
1200
1000
62

62

MAP 55

boggy!

N

OL 18

BRYN
CADER
FANER
(stone
circle)

1248 ft

55 UK

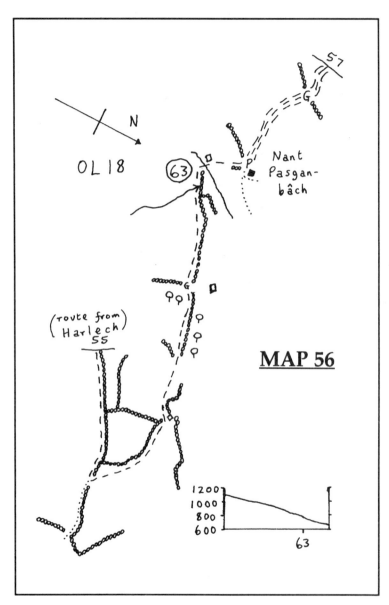

N

OL 18

⟨63⟩

Nant
Pasgan-
bâch

57

G

P

(route from)
Harlech
55

MAP 56

1200
1000
800
600

63

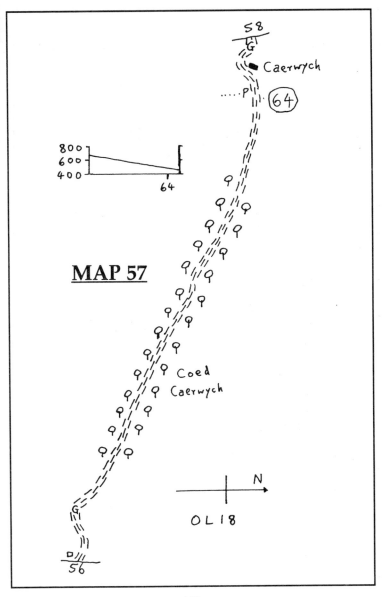

MAP 57

Caerwych

Coed Caerwych

N

OL 18

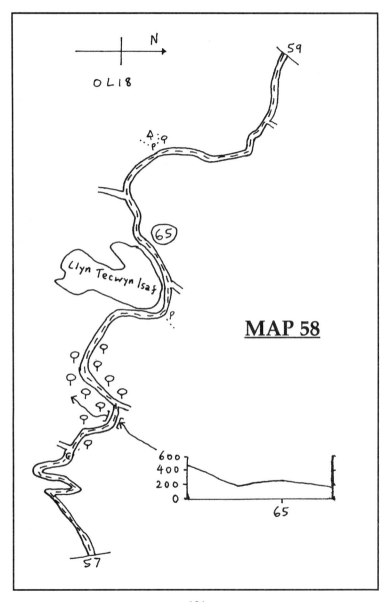

N

OL18

59

65

Llyn Tecwyn Isaf

MAP 58

600
400
200
0

65

57

200
0
66

MAP 59

Penrhyndeudraeth

Afon
Dwyryd

LLANDECWYN STATION

(66)

Grid Ref.: SH 618 379

Machynlleth

A496
Maentwrog

Bus

A496

Harlech

P

P...

58

N

OL18

Llandecwyn – Porthmadog

It's well worth diverting to Port Meirion (between miles 68 and 69). This Italianate village is the realisation of a vision of the architect Sir Clough Williams-Ellis. This secluded spot was bought in 1925 and Sir Clough's creation was complete in 1972, six years before his death at the age of 95. The buildings are intended to enhance the countryside, not spoil it. Noel Coward wrote *Blithe Spirit* here, while the television series *The Prisoner* was located here. There is an admission fee for day visitors (it's also possible to stay here).

Just after mile 69 is Penrhyn-isaf. On 7 September, 1812, Thomas Edwards (Hwntw Mawr) murdered the maid, Mary Jones. Mary was just 18, the eldest of eight children. She lies buried at Llanfrothen. The murderer, who was a construction worker on the Cob, was aged 69 and had stolen £35 and a watch. Hanged at Dolgellau on 7 April, 1813, his body was dissected.

The Ffestiniog Railway enables rail journeys to be made from the Cambrian Coast Line to the Conwy Valley Line. Minffordd is the interchange. Boston Lodge Works is built on the site of the quarry that supplied stone for constructing the Cob. The Cob opened in 1811 as part of William Madocks' plan to reclaim land, build a town and create a ferry-port for Ireland.

Slate from Ffestiniog was exported from Porthmadog, hence the opening of the narrow-gauge Ffestiniog Railway in 1836. Steam engines replaced horses in 1863 and passenger trains were introduced in 1865.

Walkers leave Meirionnydd as they cross the Cob to reach Porthmadog, where there is a station on the Cambrian Coast Line and a terminus of the Welsh Highland Railway. The Meirionnydd Coast Walk also meets John Cantrell's Lleyn Peninsula Coastal Path in Porthmadog.

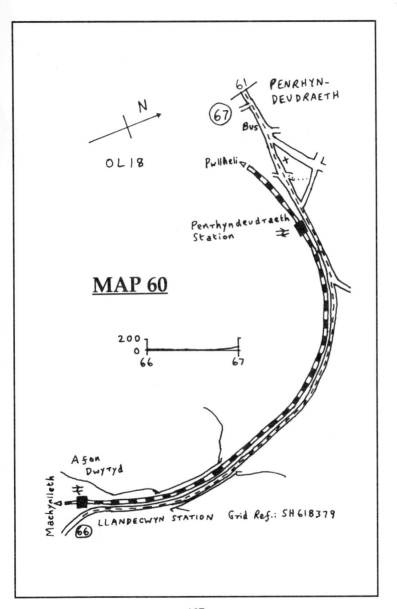

N

OL 18

MAP 60

61
67
Bus

PENRHYN-
DEUDRAETH

Pwllheli

L

Penrhyndeudraeth
Station

200
0
66   67

Afon
Dwyryd

Machynlleth

LLANDECWYN STATION   Grid Ref.: SH 618379

66

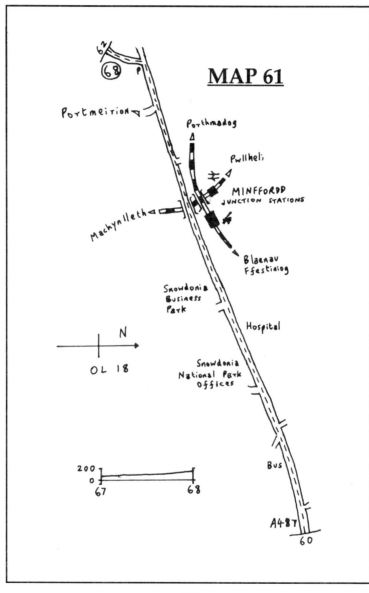

MAP 61

Portmeirion

Porthmadog

Pwllheli

MINFFORDD
JUNCTION STATIONS

Machynlleth

Blaenau
Ffestiniog

Snowdonia
Business
Park

Hospital

N

OL 18

Snowdonia
National Park
Offices

Bus

200
0
67   68

A487
60

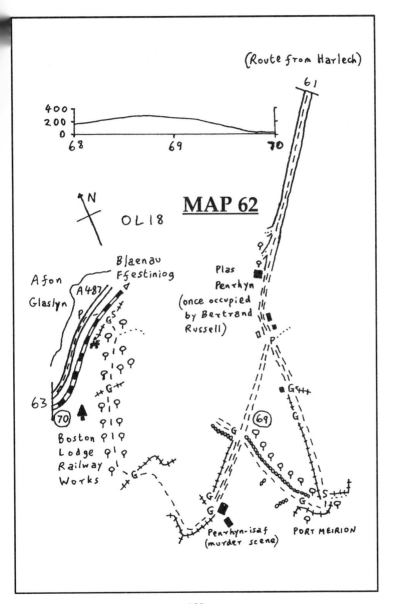

(Route from Harlech)

61

MAP 62

OL 18

N

Blaenau
Ffestiniog

A fon
Glaslyn

A 487

Plas
Penrhyn
(once occupied
by Bertrand
Russell)

P

G

63

70

Boston
Lodge
Railway
Works

G

69

G

G

Penrhyn-isaf
(murder scene)

PORT MEIRION

G

S

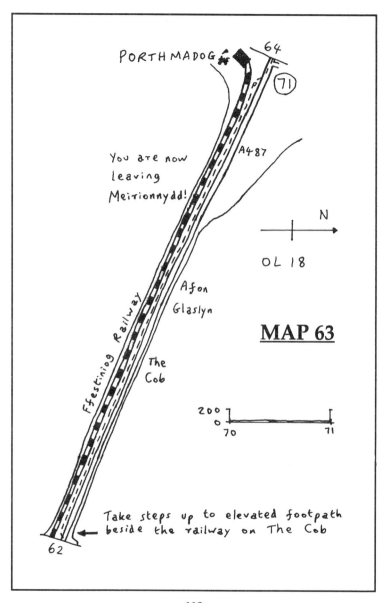

PORTHMADOG

64

(71)

A487

You are now
leaving
Meirionnydd!

N

OL 18

Afon
Glaslyn

MAP 63

Ffestiniog Railway

The
Cob

200
0
70   71

Take steps up to elevated footpath
beside the railway on The Cob

62

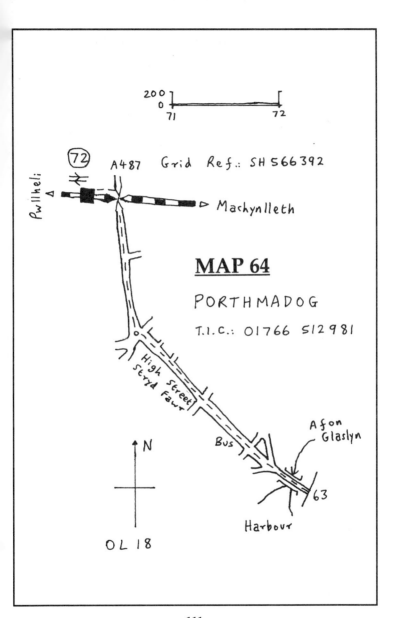

MAP 64

PORTHMADOG

T.I.C.: 01766 512981

OL 18

Walking the Way – Transport and Accommodation

The scenic Cambrian Coast railway is the ideal form of transport to gain access to the Meirionnydd Coast Walk. Trains run between Pwllheli and Machynlleth, with some through trains continuing to Shrewsbury and Birmingham. Telephone 08457 484950 for details. Gwynedd also has a good bus network (tel. 0870 6082608). The Talyllyn Railway's' phone no is 01654 710472, the Fairbourne Railway is on 01341 250362 and the Ffestiniog Railway's is 01766 512340. If you wish to take a ride on the Welsh Highland Railway when you reach Porthmadog, telephone 01766 513402.

All types of accommodation abound along this route. There is one youth hostel, at Llanbedr (tel. 01341 241287). Hostellers could base themselves here and take the train from Llanbedr to walk this route in a series of day-trips. Membership details are available from the YHA, Trevelyan House, 8 St Stephen's Hill, St Alban's, Herts, AL1 2DY, tel. 01727 855215.

If you are camping, invaluable help (including the best sites guide and map) comes with membership of the Camping & Caravaning Club, Greenfields House, Westwood Way, Coventry, CV4 8JH, tel.01203 694995. I camped at Min-y-Don, Harlech (tel. 01766 780286).

Details of hotels and B&Bs are available from local TICs. These are: Aberdyfi tel. 01654 767321, Tywyn 01654 710070, Barmouth 01341 280787, Harlech 01766 780658 and Porthmadog 01766 512981. The Wales Tourist Board's 'phone no is 02920 499909. CADW (Heritage in Wales) offer season tickets. For details, tel. 02920 500200.

Help preserve our network of public footpaths and bridleways and enjoy them in the company of others by joining the Ramblers' Association. Contact the Ramblers in Wales at Tŷ'r Cerddwyr, High Street, Gresford, Wrexham, LL12 8PT, tel. 01978 855148.

The Long Distance Walkers' Association furthers the interests of those who enjoy long distance walking. Their handbook contains a directory of long distance paths, showing how this route can be linked to others (such as the Dyfi Valley Way). Contact the LDWA's secretary, Tom Sinclair, at Bank House, High Street, Wrotham, Sevenoaks, Kent, TN15 7AE, tel. 01732 883705.

Remember the Country Code!

Enjoy the countryside and respect it.
Guard against all risk of fire.
Leave gates as you find them.
Keep dogs under close control.
Keep to public paths across farmland.
Use gates and stiles to cross fences, hedges and walls.
Leave livestock, crops and machinery alone.
Take your litter home.
Help to keep all water clean.
Protect wildlife, plants and trees.
Take special care on country roads.
Make no unnecessary noise.

Key to the Strip Map

⑨	The footpath route, with distance walked from Aberdyfi in miles
4	Number of preceding or following map
......	Other paths
⫽	Motor roads
====	Partly-metalled lanes
▭▬	Railway line
▬	Station on Cambrian Coast Line
▬	Station on narrow gauge railway
+++++	Fence or hedge
ᵒᵒᵒᵒᵒᵒᵒ	Wall
o	Standing stone
ᵒᵒᵒ	Stone circle
⛫	Castle
+	Church or chapel
△ 1200ft	Summit (with height)

Each map has a gradient profile

Key to the Strip Map continued

G	Gate
S	Stile
P	Signpost
⟿	Stream or river with direction of flow
⤙⤚	Bridge
△ ♀	Trees
▪ ▮	Buildings
▫	Ruin
✗	Campsite
Bus	Bus stop
🛖	Cromlech (burial chamber)
N ↗	Direction of North (N.B. varies from map to map, so DO CHECK!)
OL 18	Number of relevant Ordnance Survey Outdoor Leisure map

Afon is Welsh for river,
Nant means stream.
The map scale is six inches to one mile.